The
NOVELTY CAKE
Book

The
NOVELTY CAKE
Book

A New Approach to Creating Spectacular Cakes

LINDSAY JOHN BRADSHAW

MEREHURST

CAKE SKILL GUIDE

Easy	Intermediate	Advanced
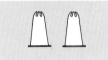		
Not too time consuming.	These take longer and require more skill.	Advanced preparation is required and involves specialist techniques.

The author and publisher would like to thank the following:

Squires Kitchen, Squires House, 3 Waverley Lane, Farnham, Surrey
GU9 8BB

Cake Art Ltd, Unit 16, Crown Close, Crown Industrial Estate,
Priorswood, Taunton, Somerset TA2 8RX

J. F. Renshaw Ltd, Mitcham House, River Court, Albert Drive,
Woking, Surrey GU21 5RP

Guinness Brewing G.B., Park Royal Brewery, London NW10 7RR

AC Sports, 780 Ormskirk Road, Pemberton, Wigan, Lancashire
WN5 8BB

The Icing Shop, 259a Orrell Road, Orrell, Wigan, Lancashire WN5 8NB

Edited by Barbara Croxford
Designed by Sue Storey
Photography by Clive Streeter

Published 1993 by Merehurst Limited
Ferry House, 51–57 Lacy Road, Putney
London SW15 1PR

Reprinted 1993

Copyright © Merehurst Limited 1993

A catalogue record for this book is available from the British Library
ISBN 1 85391 055 4

Typeset by J&L Composition Ltd, UK
Colour separation by Koford International, Singapore
Printed by Leefung–Asco Printers Ltd, Hong Kong

CONTENTS

CAKE MAKING

Good novelty cake work relies on a good base to start with; it is no use working with crumbly cake otherwise layering and shaping can be difficult and untidy. Madeira is a firm, close textured cake, ideal for cutting and shaping. Swiss roll has its uses where cylindrical forms are required. Truffle paste is invaluable for those awkward, intricate shapes so often a part of novelty cakes.

LINING TINS (PANS)

Neat lining of tins prevents cake mixture from sticking and helps to ensure a good shape.

Square, Rectangular and Swiss Roll Tins (Jelly Roll Pans) Place the tin (pan) on a piece of greaseproof paper (parchment) and draw around the base. Cut around the shape, leaving a 2.5cm (1inch) margin all round, 5cm (2inch) for deep tins. Cut diagonally in from the corners to the marked lines. Brush the tin with fat, then press the paper into the tin so that the cut corners overlap. Grease the paper.

Round and Sandwich Tins (Pans) Brush sandwich tins (layer pans) with melted fat and base line with greaseproof paper (parchment).

For deep tins (pans) the sides need lining. Cut a piece of greaseproof paper long enough to go around the cake tin side and to the depth of the tin, plus 2.5cm (1inch) deeper. Make a 2.5cm (1inch) fold along the length of the paper; snip at intervals between the edge of the paper and fold. Brush the sides and base of the tin with fat, place the paper into position around the side of the tin with the snipped edge lying flat on the base. Place the base paper in, then grease the paper.

MADEIRA CAKE

1 Preheat the oven to 160°C (325°F/Gas 3). In a warm bowl, cream the butter and sugar with the lemon rind, using either a wooden spoon or an electric mixer. When ready, the mixture will be pale in colour and light and fluffy in consistency.

2 Gradually add the eggs, beating well between each addition. Add a little flour, if necessary, to prevent curdling.

3 Sift the flours together into a bowl. Sift again into the creamed mixture, adding about one third at a time, folding carefully with a large metal spoon. Cut through to the bottom of the bowl

A variety of tin shapes and sizes for cake making.

6

Madeira Cake Quantities Chart

Cake tin (pan) size	13cm (5inch) ROUND	15cm (6inch) ROUND	15cm (6inch) SQUARE 15cm (6inch) HALF SPHERE	18cm (7inch) SQUARE 20 × 15cm (8 × 6inch) OVAL	20cm (8inch) SQUARE 20cm (8inch) HALF SPHERE	25cm (10inch) SQUARE	28cm (11inch) SQUARE
butter, softened	60g (2oz/$\frac{1}{4}$ cup)	125g (4oz/$\frac{1}{2}$ cup)	185g (6oz/$\frac{3}{4}$ cup)	250g (8oz/1 cup)	315g (10oz/1$\frac{1}{4}$ cups)	375g (12oz/1$\frac{1}{2}$ cups)	440g (14oz/1$\frac{3}{4}$ cups)
caster (superfine) sugar	60g (2oz/$\frac{1}{4}$ cup)	125g (4oz/$\frac{1}{2}$ cup)	185g (6oz/$\frac{3}{4}$ cup)	250g (8oz/1 cup)	315g (10oz/1$\frac{1}{4}$ cups)	375g (12oz/1$\frac{1}{2}$ cups)	440g (14oz/1$\frac{3}{4}$ cups)
grated rind and juice of lemon	$\frac{1}{4}$	$\frac{1}{2}$	$\frac{3}{4}$	1	1$\frac{1}{4}$	1$\frac{1}{2}$	1$\frac{3}{4}$
eggs, beaten (weighed)	75g (2$\frac{1}{2}$oz)	125g (4oz)	250g (8oz)	315g (10oz)	375g (12oz)	440g (14oz)	500g (1lb)
self raising flour	50g (1$\frac{3}{4}$oz/7tbsp)	90g (3oz/$\frac{3}{4}$ cup)	155g (5oz/1$\frac{1}{4}$ cups)	220g (7oz/1$\frac{3}{4}$ cups)	280g (9oz/2$\frac{1}{4}$ cups)	345g (11oz/2$\frac{3}{4}$ cups)	410g (13oz/3$\frac{1}{4}$ cups)
plain (all-purpose) flour	20g ($\frac{3}{4}$oz/3tbsp)	30g (1oz/$\frac{1}{4}$ cup)	60g (2oz/$\frac{1}{2}$ cup)	90g (3oz/$\frac{3}{4}$ cup)	125g (4oz/1cup)	155g (5oz/1$\frac{1}{4}$ cups)	185g (6oz/1$\frac{1}{2}$ cups)
*Cocoa (unsweetened) powder (optional)	15g ($\frac{1}{2}$oz/2tbsp)	15g ($\frac{1}{2}$oz/2tbsp)	30g (1oz/$\frac{1}{4}$ cup)	30g (1oz/$\frac{1}{4}$ cup)	45g (1$\frac{1}{2}$oz/6tbsp)	45g (1$\frac{1}{2}$oz/6tbsp)	60g (2oz/$\frac{1}{2}$ cup)
BAKING TIME (approximate depending on oven)	45mins–1 hour	1–1$\frac{1}{4}$ hours	1$\frac{1}{4}$–1$\frac{1}{2}$ hours	1$\frac{1}{2}$–1$\frac{3}{4}$ hours	1$\frac{3}{4}$–2hours	2–2$\frac{1}{4}$ hours	2$\frac{1}{4}$–2$\frac{1}{2}$ hours

* If using cocoa (unsweetened) powder to make a chocolate Madeira, omit the lemon rind and juice, and substitute the same weight of plain (all-purpose) flour with cocoa.

with a figure-of-eight movement. Add sufficient lemon juice to make a soft dropping consistency. If more liquid is needed, add water or milk.

4 Transfer the mixture to the prepared tin (pan). See the chart for baking times. Cover the cake with greaseproof paper (parchment) after about 1 hour to prevent overbrowning.

5 When baked, a warm skewer inserted into the cake should come out clean. Cool in the tin, then invert onto a wire rack.

SWISS ROLL

INGREDIENTS
90g (3oz/⅓ cup) caster (superfine) sugar
3 eggs
90g (3oz/¾ cup) plain (all-purpose) flour
½ tsp baking powder

1 Preheat the oven to 220°C (425°F/Gas 7). Combine the sugar and eggs in a heatproof bowl. Whisk over hot water until the mixture is very thick, pale and creamy. When the whisk is lifted, its trail should be visible on the surface of the mixture for a few seconds. Remove the bowl from the heat and continue whisking for 3–5 minutes more.

2 Sift the flour and baking powder together onto a sheet of greaseproof paper (parchment). Sift again over the surface of the mixture. Gently fold in, using a figure-of-eight movement to ensure that all flour has been incorporated. Take care not to overbeat or the mixture will deflate.

3 Pour the mixture into the prepared tin (pan) and carefully spread level using a palette knife. Bake at once for 7–9 minutes, until firm to the touch. Invert the baked sponge onto caster (superfine) sugar dusted greaseproof paper (parchment) and remove the lining paper.

SHAPING
Trim the edges of the roll, spread with jam and roll up tightly. If using a buttercream filling, roll up the roll with a sheet of waxed paper inside. Allow to cool, then unroll and spread with buttercream before re-rolling.

By rolling from the long side a conventional sized roll will be produced. Rolling from the short side will produce a shorter but thicker roll. For large cake shapes join two together.

The long shape of a Swiss roll lends itself particularly well to many novelty cakes, in many instances forming the basic structure on which to build. Apart from being useful as a base shape, by cutting and joining pieces of Swiss roll into certain configurations you save much time shaping and layering than you would using conventional square and round cakes. As with other types of cake, it is advisable to freeze the cake for a short period prior to shaping, making cutting and sculpting easier. Join the cakes using jam, buttercream or melted chocolate.

CHOCOLATE
Substitute 15g (½oz/2tbsp) flour with cocoa (unsweetened cocoa) powder.

HINT

To obtain a perfectly shaped roll, wrap a sheet of greaseproof paper (parchment) tightly around the roll and allow to stand like this until ready for use.

Swiss roll can be cut and joined to good effect.

TRUFFLE PASTE

A firm paste ideal for moulding and shaping, being particularly useful for difficult to shape pieces and sections on certain novelty cakes.

INGREDIENTS
500g (1lb/8 cups) cake crumbs (see Note)
60g (2oz/⅓ cup) apricot jam
60ml (2fl oz/¼ cup) evaporated milk
½ tsp vanilla essence (extract)
about 125g (4oz) melted chocolate (see Note)

1 Place the cake crumbs in a bowl, add the apricot jam, evaporated milk and essence.

2 Mix the ingredients a little using a spoon, then stream in the melted chocolate and continue mixing until a firm paste is formed. (A dry mix will crumble and be difficult to mould, while a mixture that is too soft will not retain its shape when moulded.)

3 The prepared mixture will keep for a few days sealed in an airtight container in the refrigerator. To create shapes, simply mould using your hands with icing (confectioner's) sugar for dusting. Attach shaped pieces to the main cake using jam, melted chocolate or buttercream.

Makes about 750g (1½lb/3 cups)

NOTE If using chocolate cake crumbs, use melted milk or plain chocolate. For plain cake crumbs, use white chocolate. The amount of chocolate required will vary depending whether the crumbs are dry or moist.

Adding melted chocolate to truffle ingredients.

Truffle paste is easy to mould into useful shapes.

CAKE TRIMMINGS
Truffle paste makes use of any cake trimmings that are left over from shaping cakes. Cake trimmings can be frozen in polythene bags and stored for subsequent use, either as they are to be used for forming shapes (see Golf Bag page 24) or crumbed and sieved for making truffle paste (see Horse page 26).

FILLINGS AND ICINGS

Novelty cakes not only need to look good, they must also taste nice. After taking time to bake your cakes, give a little thought to the most suitable creams, icing, chocolate and colourings you intend to use to assemble and decorate the cake. This section provides recipes, methods and useful advice to help you make your choice.

BUTTERCREAM

Used in each recipe to sandwich cakes together adding an extra dimension in flavour, appearance and moistness to the cake, buttercream is also spread thinly onto cakes as an adhesive medium for the sugarpaste covering.

INGREDIENTS
185g (6oz/¾ cup) butter, softened
2 tbsp milk
375g (12oz/3 cups) icing (confectioner's) sugar
flavouring

1 Place the softened butter in a large bowl. Gradually add the milk, working the mixture together until creamy. For a less rich filling, a soft butter and quality margarine mixture may be used, in which case less liquid will be required.

2 Sift the icing (confectioner's) sugar and gradually stir into the butter. Beat hard with a wooden spoon or electric mixer until pale, light and fluffy. A little extra liquid may be needed if a soft icing is required.

HINT

The decorative mediums described are the basic ones and most often used, however, there are numerous edible materials that can be utilized. Experiment with piping jelly, liquorice, toffees (candies), marshmallow and rice (wafer) paper to make special features on your cakes.

FLAVOURINGS
Citrus Add the juice and finely grated rind of oranges, lemons or limes.
Chocolate Add melted bitter dessert chocolate or cocoa (unsweetened cocoa) powder mixed to a paste with a little hot water and chilled before adding to the cream.
Coffee Chill freshly filtered strong black coffee – add to taste.
Almond Use almond essence (extract) sparingly to taste.
Liqueur Use Grand Marnier, Kirsch, Tia Maria, Cointreau, Maraschino. Rum and brandy may also be used sparingly.

ROYAL ICING

15g (½oz) albumen powder or albumen based powder
90ml (3fl oz/⅓ cup) water
500g (1lb/4 cups) icing (confectioner's) sugar, finely sieved

1 Prepare the albumen powder with water, according to the manufacturer's instructions. Strain the solution into a bowl.

2 Add half the sugar, mixing well with a wooden spatula or spoon. Add the remaining sugar and continue mixing until all the icing sugar is incorporated. Scrape down the sides of the bowl, then lightly beat the mixture by hand or machine until a definite bold peak is left when lifted with a spatula.

USES FOR ROYAL ICING

Use this icing for piping the decorative borders, lettering, basketweave and fine detail on the cakes. A stippled effect can be created by applying the icing using a small piece of foam sponge. Also use royal icing for attaching and joining sugarpaste, pastillage and other pieces to the cakes.

COLOURINGS

A wider variety of edible food colourings than ever before is now available. They come in liquid and paste form, powder and pens (page 19).

Liquid colouring Liquid colours are suitable only for producing pastel tints. If using such a weak colour solution, avoid trying to produce very dark shades as the amount of liquid usually required renders the royal icing (or sugarpaste) too soft to work with.

Paste colouring Available in a comprehensive range of colours. They are regarded as the best to use for colouring sugarpaste and royal icing. Use the tip of a cocktail stick (toothpick) to add the colour in small amounts until the desired tint or shade is produced.

Dusting powder (petal dust/blossom tint)
As the name implies, this type of colour is mainly used in novelty cake work for dusting colour onto sugarpaste or royal icing to create interesting effects. It is also used to tint leaves and the centres or petal edges of flowers. It can be used to colour royal icing, but as the intensity is not very strong it is uneconomical to use in large quantities.

Chocolate, buttercream and coloured sugarpaste.

CHOCOLATE

Chocolate can be used in novelty cake work for joining cakes and sections of cake together, or spread or piped as a cake or board covering or decoration. Several types are suitable, from couverture, the purest form which needs to be tempered (heated and cooled several times to precise temperatures) before use, to baker's coating chocolate which is easily melted over a pan of hot water or in a microwave. Chocolate flavoured cake covering can be used, as can chocolate chips which are useful as a decoration or to represent soil, gravel paths and other effects.

DESIGNING NOVELTY CAKES

Although a varied selection of cakes suitable for different occasions, events and personalities is provided, you will no doubt at some time in your cake decorating want to design and create your adaptation or unique and original idea.

After hitting on an idea you feel would work well as a novelty cake, you need to research any information you will require. It may be that you need a children's magazine to adapt a character or model from, or you may need drawings or photographs showing differing angles of the item or person to be sculpted in cake. A word of caution here, for your own personal use copying is usually acceptable, but for commercially produced cakes you must first seek the permission of the copyright owner.

A simple card template aids cutting unusual shapes.

Having collated the information you require, you then need to plan the basic cake shape and decide which is the most economical way to form the cake. It may be that you can build it up from basic round, square or rectangular cakes, you may use Swiss roll or truffle paste (page 9) to mould and form intricate shapes. Special shapes can be cut from a piece of cake with the aid of a template as shown. Also take into account, at this stage, any problems that may be encountered with difficult shapes such as covering or supporting.

Once the basic cake shape is confirmed, you then need to assess the practicalities of decoration. An understanding of the characteristics of various pieces of equipment, creams, icings, pastes, colourings and decorative techniques is essential at this stage; a skill level is assumed but if in doubt refer to the appropriate section for information.

Next make a simple drawing or sketch showing the outline of the basic cake shapes to be used, along with the relevant measurements. Add to this notes about cake board size, fillings, icings and colourings to be used. You can colour the sketch simply using crayons or pencils, just to give an impression of how the finished cake will appear. Finally list the equipment you will need, in particular any specialist items, this will act as a checklist to consult before commencing work.

Also make any templates you need from the designs and sketches you have made, then simply cut the shapes from thin card. If you need to dry any pastillage shapes in special positions, make a 'former' from thin card or suitably sized card tubes from kitchen paper etc. (see page 15).

HINT

Don't attempt to decorate a cake that is beyond your level of skill. It is far better to make a neat finish to a simple novelty than to struggle to perfect a more intricate design.

CUTTING AND LAYERING

Preparation of the cake is a most important part of novelty cake work. Careful handling, even cutting and neat layering all contribute to making an accurate cake base on which to build and also provide a visually pleasing appearance to the cake when cut.

Ideally cakes should be stored (not refrigerated) for approximately 12 hours before commencing work with them and particularly before cutting, when cool just wrap them loosely in a polythene sheet. This storage period allows the crumb to close a little and the cake as a whole to firm up, thus enabling easier handling.

Before cutting, layering or creaming of any kind takes place, it is normal practice to remove the thin crust or 'skin' from the top of the cake by drawing the back edge of a long knife across the cake, or use a sharp serrated knife in a conventional manner.

To achieve even and accurate slicing, which will help towards good layering, use two pieces of wood as shown or commercially available polypropylene cutting boards. Place a board at each side of the cake, hold the cake steady and using a sharp knife resting on the boards, cut through the cakes.

Whilst working always keep the cake covered and in particular any cut surfaces, to prevent loss of moisture leading to drying of the cake. A good method is to slide the cake into a large polythene bag.

Once cut the cakes can be spread with even layers of jam or buttercream, or you may prefer to use one of the fillings only.

Using cutting boards ensures a neat and level cut.

Spread the buttercream evenly for good layering.

HINT

Place the layered cake into the refrigerator for about 45 minutes to firm; this will make shaping easier and prevent the cake crumbling. Intricate shapes can be sculpted easier by first freezing the layered cake and then allowing to thaw slightly.

COVERING CAKES AND BOARDS

HINT

Crimping tools, available from sugarcraft shops, can be used to easily and quickly create a decorative edge on sugarpaste and in particular covered cake boards.

The sugarpaste referred to in each recipe for covering the cakes and boards is commercially available in a ready-to-roll form. You can buy the paste white allowing you to produce your own colours, or purchase it ready coloured in a limited but popular range of tints as shown on page 11.

COLOURING SUGARPASTE

To colour the sugarpaste simply add colouring (page 11) and knead through until evenly distributed. Keep any unused sugarpaste sealed in polythene while working and in particular during storage.

COVERING CAKES

Having coloured the paste it is ready to roll out, using white paste from scratch will require a short kneading time to soften the paste and make it more pliable. By now the cake will have been prepared as described on page 13 and in the appropriate novelty cake shape. Next cover the cake with a thin spreading of buttercream to act as an adhesive for the sugarpaste. Roll out the sugarpaste on a clean flat surface, such as a kitchen worktop or a large cutting board, use icing (confectioner's) sugar for rolling out. Pick up the paste by sliding your hands (palms uppermost) underneath and lift onto the cake. Carefully take your hands away allowing the paste to drape loosely over the cake. Slightly curve one hand and use to tease the paste smoothly over the cake, removing creases and folds as you go. Trim off any excess paste from the base using a small knife, then use a smoother or flat plastic scraper to make

HINT

Using the board covering method described, removing the cake shaped portion, will prevent the base of the cake coming into direct contact with the sugarpaste which can cause the sugarpaste to discolour and sweat.

a clean, neat, flawless surface. Set the cake aside or transfer onto a cake board ready for decoration.

COVERING BOARDS

Covering cake boards uses the same method as described for cakes, except the cake board is very lightly moistened with water to stick the sugarpaste on. Trim off excess sugarpaste using a small knife. The board can be covered fully. Alternatively, you may prefer to make a template of the cake shape and cut away the area of sugarpaste as shown before placing the cake on and securing with dabs of royal icing. If the board edge is to be decorated using a crimping tool (see Hint), this should be done now while the sugarpaste is still soft.

To give a more finished look to your cakes, attach a suitably coloured ribbon or silver or gold paper banding to the board edge, using non-toxic adhesive, at the last stage of decoration.

Removing the cake shaped portion of sugarpaste.

WORKING WITH PASTILLAGE

A firm pliable paste which is moulded or rolled and cut into the desired shape, then dried until firm. Pastillage is readily available commercially as a powdered mix to which water is added. Alternatively, you can produce your own using the recipe.

500g (1lb/4 cups) icing (confectioner's) sugar
½ tsp gum tragacanth
1½ tsp powdered gelatine (unflavored gelatin)
60ml (2fl oz/¼ cup) water

1. Sift the icing (confectioner's) sugar and gum tragacanth together into an ovenproof bowl. Place the mixture in the oven at 150°C (300°F/Gas 2) for about 10 minutes until warm. Alternatively, stand the bowl in a sink of very hot water until warmed.

2. Sprinkle the gelatine over the water in a small bowl. Leave to soften for 10 minutes until sponged. Stand the bowl over a saucepan of hot (not boiling) water and stir the gelatine until dissolved.

3. Add the gelatine to the icing sugar, then beat using an electric mixer until white and pliable. Knead the paste together by hand. Makes about 500g (1lb).

NOTE: Pastillage should be stored in a polythene bag and placed in an airtight container, then left for 24 hours before use.

Use formers to dry particular shapes of pastillage.

COLOURING

Use either liquid colours or non-glycerine paste colours so that the drying and hardening qualities of the pastillage are not affected. Colours which contain glycerine obviously attract moisture, therefore extending the drying time and preventing the pastillage setting completely hard. If in any doubt, and to ensure success, cut the required shapes from white pastillage and paint or dust them with colour when dry.

TEMPLATES

Make templates from the drawings provided, cutting the shapes out of thin card. On a surface dusted with icing (confectioner's) sugar, roll out the pastillage to the required thickness. Place the card templates on top and carefully cut out the required pastillage shapes. Leave to dry and turn the shapes over halfway through drying if necessary.

HINT

TEXTURES To create interesting detail on pastillage you can use a variety of implements and tools, such as textured rolling pins (page 18), modelling tools, cutters and piping tubes (tips).

FORMERS Drying pastillage shapes in particular positions requires suitably shaped household objects or formers specially made from cardboard tubes, boxes or polystyrene fruit trays. Always cover the object or former with waxed paper to prevent the pastillage sticking.

SPECIAL EFFECTS

A book entirely devoted to making novelty cakes will inevitably feature numerous textures and effects. To avoid repetition, the various methods are illustrated and described here. Simply refer back to this section.

MODELLING

All the effects can be made using sugarpaste or marzipan (almond paste).

Stone Cut out irregular shaped rectangles of stone coloured sugarpaste, attach to the iced cake surface by moistening with water. Fill the joins with mortar coloured royal icing using tube (tip) no. 2.

Soil Use a clay gun to create 'crumbs' of dark brown coloured marzipan or sugarpaste. Moisten the surface to be decorated and place the soil evenly on.

Sand Colour caster (superfine) sugar with paprika liquid or paste colouring, allow to dry naturally on a paper lined tray. Sprinkle onto soft royal icing or moistened sugarpaste.

Brick Make using cut out rectangles of brick coloured sugarpaste, or use a textured brickwork rolling pin overleaf. Colour with orange and red dusting powder, then fill the joins with cement coloured royal icing using tube (tip) no. 2.

Rocks Blend light brown and grey coloured marzipan or sugarpaste together, do not thoroughly mix. Cut into pieces and roll into irregular shapes.

Cobbles Make as described previously for rocks, then flatten out and attach to the cake by moistening with water.

Sea and water Coat the cake board with deep blue coloured sugarpaste as described on page 14. While still soft, push indents in the paste with a thumb at regular intervals. Use a no. 2 sable paint brush to brush on white royal icing surf. Allow to dry, then glaze with confectioner's varnish to create a wet look.

Marble Mix small amounts of coloured sugarpaste into a larger amount of a paler coloured sugarpaste, do not mix thoroughly. Roll out to create the desired marble effect. Streaks of colour can also be painted on using a fine paint brush.

Roof tiles Colour sugarpaste to the desired colour and roll out thinly. Use a small round cutter to make the shapes then arrange as shown, overlapping each row. When dry, colour the roof tiles with orange, red and brown dusting powders.

Windows Make a suitable background colour for the window, then place a piece of leaf gelatine, cut to the same size, over the shape. Edge with strips of brown sugarpaste to form the window frame.

Tree bark Roll out some brown sugarpaste thinly and attach to the cake or board. Using the back of a knife, make close lines. Roll a thin spiral of sugarpaste and attach then flatten to create a wood knot. Colour the tree bark with brown dusting powder.

Samples of effects used on the featured cakes (and overleaf). From the top left to right: Stone; Soil and Sand; Brick; Rocks and Cobbles; Sea and Water; Marble; Roof tiles; Windows; Tree bark.

HINT

Almost all the special effects can be achieved using conventional kitchen utensils. However, as you become more proficient it is wise to invest in various modelling tools, embossers and cutters to make the work easier, quicker and more professional.

More Special Effects for novelty cakes. From left to right: Grass; Wood grain; Gravel.

Grass   Cover the cake or board (page 14) with green coloured sugarpaste. Either stipple using a piece of foam sponge with browny-green royal icing or use a clay gun to force out small thin tufts of browny-green coloured sugarpaste. A simpler method of creating grass would be to follow the method described on page 16 for sand, replacing the paprika colour with green.

Wood grain   Colour sugarpaste to the required wood effect tint and use to cover the cake or board. When dry, use a fine paint brush or a food colour pen to paint or draw fine brown lines and an occasional knot.

Gravel   Roll out some grey coloured sugarpaste and, using a small knife, cut into very thin strips. Cut again at right angles and to the same width to make tiny cubes of paste. Accuracy isn't as important as irregularity creates a more natural effect.

TEXTURED ROLLING PINS

Used to texture large areas of sugarpaste, pastillage or marzipan, there are three commercially available ones: ribbed (parallel lines) sometimes referred to as smocking; boxwood (crossed lines); and basketweave.

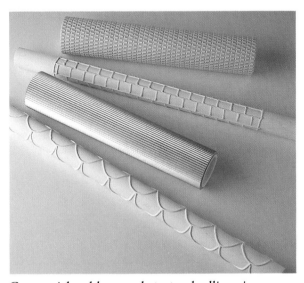

Commercial and homemade textured rolling pins.

The brickwork and roof slate designs shown are easily made by marking out a short length of dowel, then using tube (tip) no. 2 with quick drying household filler, pipe the lines on. When dry, paint with non-toxic paint to seal.

Each rolling pin is simple to use, just roll out sugarpaste using a conventional rolling pin to just more than the required thickness, then for the final roll use the selected textured pin.

PAINTING

Paste and Liquid Many of the cakes described require the technique of painting. All you need is a selection of either paste or liquid food colourings, a few sable paint brushes of varying thickness and a paint palette or dinner plate on which to mix the colours. If you wish, you can paint with the colours just mixed with water to obtain the required tint. However, you may prefer to add an edible white base powder (available from sugarcraft shops) to make a more solid colour which is also easier to control on sugarpaste, pastillage and the like.

Dusting powders (petal dust/blossom tint) Available in a continually expanding range of colours, use dusting powders to add interesting coloured tints and shades to sugarpaste. Simply brush on using a medium soft bristled brush.

Food colour pens An invaluable aid to novelty cake work, food colour pens are available in a wide range of colours. They can be used to draw, write and outline fine detail on sugarpaste, pastillage and rice (wafer) paper.

Metallic powders Available both in non-edible form for decoration only and edible for painting, dusting and mixing into sugarpaste. To get the best metallic effect, paint rather than dust, by

Liquid, paste and powder colours and pens.

Metallic powder colourings, gold leaf and dragees.

mixing the powder with water or clear alcohol (gin or vodka). Edible gold leaf is also available in small sheets.

19

PUSSY CAT

CAKE
15cm (6inch) round Madeira cake (page 6)
20 × 15cm (8 × 6inch) oval Madeira cake
470g (15oz/2 cups) buttercream (page 10)
315g (10oz/1 cup) jam for filling
DECORATION
2kg 500g (5lb) white sugarpaste
paste food colourings – green, cream, pink, red, black
90g (3oz/¾ cup) royal icing (page 10)
liquorice laces
EQUIPMENT
38 × 33cm (15 × 13inch) oval cake board
no. 3 sable paint brush

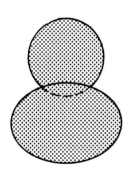

1 Prepare and layer both cakes (page 13), then cut and join as shown opposite. Cover the cake with a thin spreading of buttercream.

2 Colour 560g (1lb 2oz) sugarpaste green and cover the board using the method described on page 14.

3 Reserve 125g (4oz) sugarpaste and colour the remainder off-white using cream food colouring. Roll out the sugarpaste and cover the cake as described on page 14. Place the cake on the prepared board.

4 Colour 22g (¾oz) sugarpaste pink, a tiny piece red and the remainder black. Using the off-white coloured trimmings and prepared colours, model the eyes, nose, mouth (red), tail and paws. Make templates from the designs provided to create the ears. Allow all these pieces to dry.

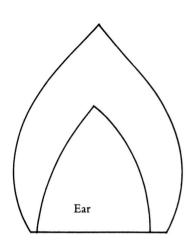
Ear

Model the eyes, nose, mouth, tail and paws.

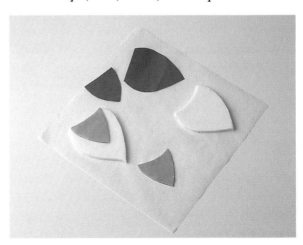
Use templates to shape the outer and inner ear.

5 Using black food colouring with a small amount of royal icing added to thicken, paint on the body markings. Attach all the prepared pieces from step 4 with royal icing and six liquorice whiskers.

YELLOW KITE

CAKE
25cm (10inch) square Madeira cake (page 6)
375g (12oz/1½ cups) buttercream (page 10)
250g (8oz/¾ cup) jam for filling
DECORATION
1kg 185g (2lb 6oz) white sugarpaste
paste food colourings – yellow, blue, red, chestnut, black
60g (2oz/½ cup) royal icing (page 10)
EQUIPMENT
40 × 30cm (16 × 12inch) oblong cake board
crimper
small oval cutter
no. 3 piping tube (tip)
30cm (12inches) blue ribbon

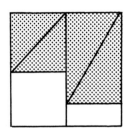

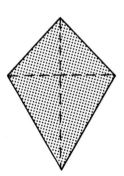

1 Prepare and layer the cake (page 13), then cut and join as shown opposite. Cover the cake completely with a thin spreading of buttercream.

2 Colour 500g (1lb) sugarpaste yellow and use to cover the cake as described on page 14.

3 Colour 500g (1lb) sugarpaste blue and cover the board as described on page 14. Make a template of the cloud design (page 80) and use the method on page 14 to make three clouds from white sugarpaste. Crimp the board edge.

4 Roll out some white sugarpaste and cut out two oval shapes for the eyes. Colour a piece of sugarpaste red and model the nose and tongue. Cut out and make the bows as shown. Colour sufficient sugarpaste chestnut to make the cross pieces. Use the remainder, coloured black, to

HINT

To make cutting and layering simpler, the diamond shape required to make the kite can be cut in one complete piece from a large cake. However, this would create considerably more cake trimmings to be re-utilized (see page 9).

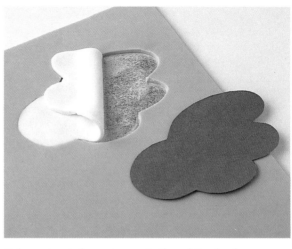

Inlay cut out shapes to create the white clouds.

Forming the bow. Template on page 80.

model the beads, mouth and eyes. Attach the pieces by lightly moistening with water. Finally pipe the mouth and eyebrows using tube (tip) no. 3 with black coloured icing. Position and attach the ribbon and bows with dabs of icing.

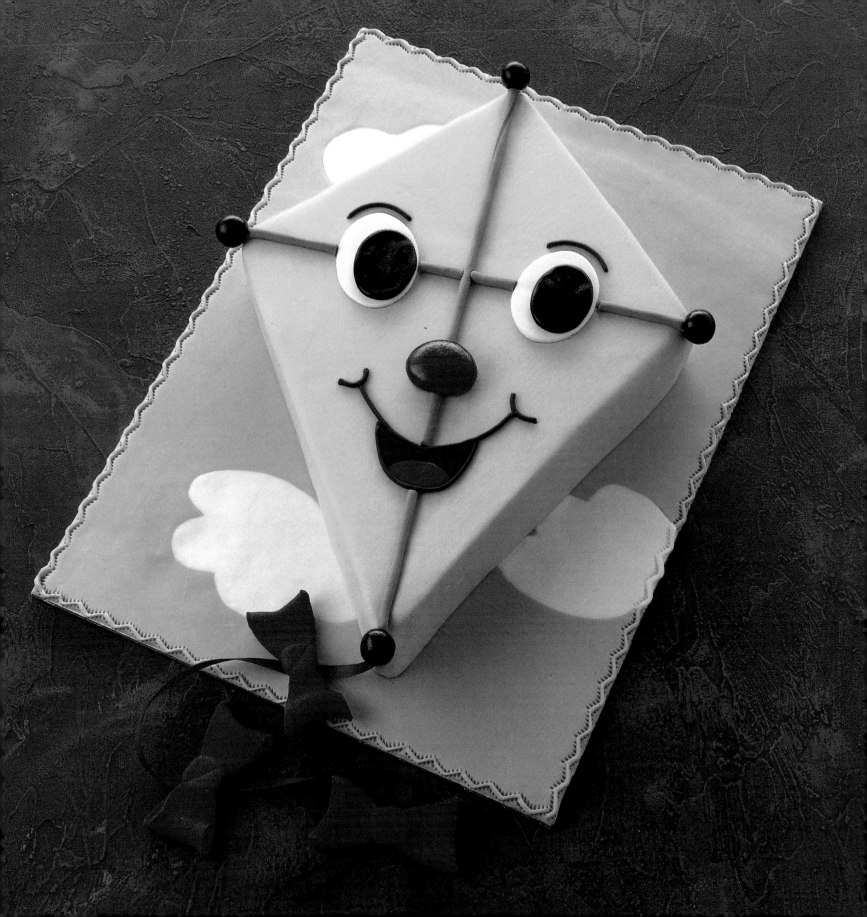

GOLF BAG

CAKE

20 × 10cm (8 × 4inch) Swiss roll (page 8)
155g (5oz/⅔ cup) buttercream (page 10)
cake trimmings/off-cuts (page 9)

DECORATION

2kg (4lb) white sugarpaste
250g (8oz) pastillage (page 15)
paste food colourings – green, brown, chestnut, red, yellow, blue
185g (6oz/1½ cups) royal icing (page 10)
silver colouring
90g (3oz/½ cup) chocolate, melted

EQUIPMENT

36cm (14inch) petal cake board
small piece of foam sponge for stippling
ball modelling tool
no. 3 sable paint brush
no. 1 piping tube (tip)

1 Prepare the cake (page 13) then stand as shown. Cover the cake with buttercream.

2 Arrange cake trimmings on the board to form a mound, attaching with dabs of buttercream. Colour 1kg 60g (2lb 2oz) sugarpaste green and cover the board, see page 14. Stipple the sugarpaste with browny-green royal icing.

3 Colour 60g (2oz) pastillage brown and roll out. Cut out a long narrow strip for the handle and allow to dry on crumpled foil to create a natural shape. Cut out three golf club heads from remaining pastillage using templates on page 79. Add the markings using a knife. Also roll out

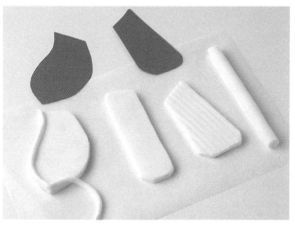

Use card templates to shape the golf club heads.

three handles – allow to dry. Attach the heads to the handles. When dry, paint silver.

4 Use the remaining white pastillage to model a golf ball, indenting the surface with a ball modelling tool. Also model some tees. Allow them to dry, then paint with food colourings.

5 Colour the remaining sugarpaste brown. Roll out and cover the cake as page 14, forming a shallow collar around the top. Use trimmings to model the pocket, moisten and attach. Secure the cake on the board with icing. Attach the prepared handle with brown icing. Pipe stitching on using tube (tip) no. 1 with pale brown icing.

6 Pour melted chocolate into the top of the golf bag then insert the golf clubs. Arrange the tees and ball and attach with icing.

HORSE

CAKE

25cm (10inch) square Madeira cake (page 6)
375g (12oz/1½ cups) buttercream (page 10)
100g (3½oz/⅓ cup) jam for filling
90g (3oz/⅓ cup) truffle paste (page 9)

DECORATION

1kg 590g (3lb 3oz) white sugarpaste
paste food colourings – egg yellow, brown, chestnut, black, pink, red
90g (3oz/¾ cup) royal icing (page 10)
gold colouring

EQUIPMENT

38 × 33cm (15 × 13inch) oval cake board
crimper
small piece of foam sponge for stippling
small round cutter
no. 3 sable paint brush

1 Make the templates on page 79. Prepare, cut the cake to shape and layer as described on page 13. Mould the truffle paste to form a shallow dome for the cheek and attach to the face with buttercream. Cover the cake completely with a thin spreading of buttercream.

2 Colour 625g (1lb 4oz) sugarpaste egg yellow and cover the board using the method described on page 14. Crimp the board edge.

3 Reserve 220g (7oz) sugarpaste and colour the remainder using brown and chestnut colouring. Roll out and cover the cake as described on page 14. Stipple the face with brown coloured royal icing.

4 Colour 125g (4oz) sugarpaste black and cut out the mane, tuft, ear and nostril. From white paste, cut out two small circles and the eye. Colour some paste pink and make the ear lining. Dry all parts. Cut narrow strips of red paste for the reigns. Attach all pieces with icing. Paint the circles with gold colouring and the eye with black.

Making the mane, tuft, ears, eye and stud.

CUP OF TEA

CAKE

two 15cm (6inch) round Madeira cakes (page 6)
15cm (6inch) diameter half sphere Madeira cake
280g (9oz/generous 1 cup) buttercream (page 10)
75g (2½oz/¼ cup) jam for filling

DECORATION

2kg 125g (4lb 4oz) white sugarpaste
250g (8oz) pastillage (page 15)
paste food colourings – cream, blue, peach, tan, green, yellow, chestnut
silver colouring
185g (6oz/1½ cups) royal icing (page 10)
30g (1oz/2tbsp) granulated sugar

EQUIPMENT

40 × 30cm (16 × 12inch) oblong cake board
two 15cm (6inch) cake boards
large spoon
23cm (9inch) diameter foil or paper plate
airbrush
no. 2 sable paint brush
round cutter
no. 3 piping tube (tip)

Prepare the modelled biscuits, spoon and handle.

For the saucer, cover a card plate with sugarpaste.

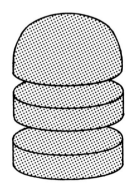

1 First prepare the handle and spoon to allow ample drying time. Roll out the pastillage and drape over the spoon, trim off excess. Model the cup handle as shown. Allow both pieces to dry completely. Paint the spoon with silver colouring.

2 Roll out 375g (12oz) sugarpaste and line the icing (confectioner's) sugar dusted plate with the paste to make the saucer, trim off the excess. Allow to dry, then paint the saucer cream colour.

3 Prepare and layer all three cakes (page 13), then join as shown opposite. Cover the cake completely with a thin spreading of buttercream.

4 Position the cake upside down on two 15cm (6inch) cake boards. Roll out 875g (1lb 12oz) sugarpaste and cover the cake (page 14) as shown here, allowing the paste to cover the cake boards to form the rim of the cup. Neatly trim off excess sugarpaste and allow to dry. Paint the cup cream colour.

HINT

If you do not have access to an airbrush, an equally attactive effect can be created by painting the sugarpaste on the cake board (page 19). To create a wet look to the tea, when dry paint the icing with confectioner's varnish.

If preferred, you can colour the sugarpaste cream before rolling out to eliminate painting.

Covering the prepared cup shape with sugarpaste.

5 Roll out 750g (1lb 8oz) sugarpaste and cover the board, using the method described on page 14. Allow to dry, then mask off with strips of paper leaving narrow spaces. Spray with blue colour using an airbrush. Remove the masking,

replace at right angles to sprayed lines and spray again to create the check tablecloth effect (see also Hint).

6 Turn the cake the right way up and remove the two boards. Make a tracing of the flower motif from the design provided and transfer onto the side of the cup. Paint the motif using a fine no. 2 paint brush with food colourings. Also paint peach coloured detail around the top of the cup, handle and saucer. Attach the handle to the cup with royal icing, then support with a small object until dry.

7 Colour the remaining sugarpaste biscuit coloured using peach and chestnut. Roll out and mark lines with a knife. Cut out two circles for the biscuits, pattern the top using tube (tip) no. 3 to make holes. Moisten the tops and press in granulated sugar; remove excess sugar.

8 Position the prepared saucer on the board and secure with icing. Position and secure the cup, spoon and biscuits. Colour the remaining royal icing tan colour and soften slightly with cold water. Spoon the icing into the cup and agitate with a spoon to make the tea; neatly level off.

Flower motif

GOLDFISH BOWL

Using the same techniques and decoration, this novelty could be made from stacked rectangular or square cakes to create an aquarium shape.

CAKE
two 20cm (8inch) diameter half sphere Madeira cakes (page 6)
280g (9oz/generous 1 cup) buttercream (page 10)
100g (3½oz/⅓ cup) jam for filling
DECORATION
1kg 625g (3lb 4oz) white sugarpaste
155g (5oz) pastillage (page 15)
paste food colourings – orange, blue, yellow, green
clear alcohol – gin or vodka
dusting powders (petal dust/blossom tint) – blue, yellow, orange
gold colouring
90g (3oz/¾ cup) royal icing (page 10)
EQUIPMENT
25cm (10inch) round cake board
small piece of soft material for ragging
curved former
no. 1 and 2 piping tubes (tips)
no. 66 leaf tube (tip)

1 Colour 375g (12oz) sugarpaste orange and roll out. Cover the cake board as described on page 14 – allow to dry.

2 Prepare and layer both cakes (page 13), then join to make a complete sphere. Cover the cake completely with a thin spreading of buttercream.

3 Colour 875g (1lb 12oz) sugarpaste blue and cover the cake using the method described on page 14. Due to the awkward shape you will need to cut a few tucks around the base and smooth the paste back together to create a neat finish. Use blue dusting powder or an airbrush with blue colouring to create a deeper blue shaded colour.

Spherical shaped cake covered with blue sugarpaste.

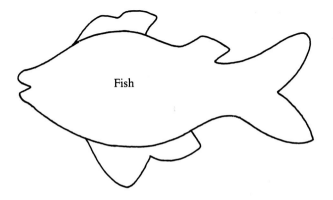

Fish

HINT

As your skills improve, you may prefer to make this cake even more colourful and interesting by making tropical fish of various shapes with detailed markings painted on using colourings.

4 On a saucer, mix a small amount of orange
colouring with little alcohol. Scrunch up a
small piece of material and use to dab the colour
randomly onto the board to create a ragging
effect. Allow to dry.

5 Make templates from the fish design. Colour
the pastillage yellow, roll out and neatly cut
out three fish shapes. Place the shapes over
a curved former to dry completely. Pipe the
detail on using tube (tip) no. 1 with yellow
royal icing. When dry, colour the fish using
yellow and orange dusting powders and gold
colouring.

Prepare the cake board and sugarpaste bowl rim.

6 Turn the cake upside down and, using leaf
tube (tip) no. 66 with green royal icing, pipe
the foliage. Turn the cake the right way and secure
onto the prepared cake board with icing.

7 Use the remaining white sugarpaste to make
the bowl rim. Roll out into two long sausage
shapes, one slightly narrower than the other.
Moisten the top of the wide roll with a little water
and attach the narrow roll on top. Shape into a
circle and attach to the cake top with icing.

8 Carefully position the fish to the side of the
bowl and attach with royal icing. Using tube
(tip) no. 2 with white royal icing, pipe the bubbles
onto the side and top of the cake.

Cut out fish shapes are dried on curved formers.

PAINT POT

The perfect cake for a DIY enthusiast. To create a realistic sheen on the paint, brush with confectioner's varnish.

CAKE
three 13cm (5inch) round Madeira cakes (page 6)
280g (9oz/generous 1 cup) buttercream (page 10)
60g (2oz/¼ cup) jam for filling
DECORATION
1kg 750g (3lb 8oz) white sugarpaste
250g (8oz) pastillage (page 15)
paste food colourings – egg yellow, chestnut, blue, purple
silver colouring
brown food colour pen
220g (7oz/1¾ cups) royal icing (page 10)
EQUIPMENT
33cm (13inch) hexagonal cake board
two 13cm (5inch) cake boards
curved former
no. 2, 3 and 8 sable paint brushes
ruler
no. 1 and 2 piping tubes (tips)

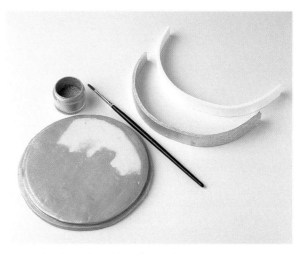

Paint the dry lid and handle with silver colouring.

A real paint brush will assist modelling detail.

1 To make the handle, roll out 60g (2oz) pastillage into a long narrow shape. Ensure that the handle fits the cake. Trim neatly with a knife and place over a curved former to dry completely. When dry, paint with silver colouring.

2 Use the remaining pastillage to model a paint brush, adding a strip to represent the metal part. For accuracy, have to hand a real paint brush or large pastry brush from which to model.

3 Prepare and layer the cakes (page 13) on top of each other to create the basic paint tin shape. Cover the cake completely with a thin spreading of buttercream.

4   For the lid, roll out 185g (6oz) sugarpaste and cut out a 13cm (5inch) round and one slightly smaller. Attach together (small on top of large) by moistening with water. Allow to dry, then paint with silver colouring.

5   Colour 750g (1lb 8oz) sugarpaste using egg yellow with a hint of chestnut. Roll out and cover the board, using the method described on page 14. Use a ruler to make equally spaced indentations across the board to represent slats of

wood – allow to dry. For the wood grain effect, use a brown food colour pen and refer to the method described on page 18.

6   Place the prepared cake centrally on the two small cake boards. Roll out the remaining white sugarpaste to a long rectangle and cover the cakes and boards by wrapping around the sides. Allow to dry, then upturn the covered cake and carefully remove the cake boards to make a rim for the tin.

7   Paint the wood grain effect (page 18) and silver detail on the pastillage paint brush, using no. 2 and 8 paint brushes. Using tube (tip) no. 1 with pale yellow royal icing, pipe the bristles.

8   Position the cake on the prepared board and attach with a dab of icing. Paint the detail on the paint tin, using a real paint tin for reference, also paint the silver rim and interior. Colour the royal icing violet and soften slightly with cold water. Spoon into the top of the cake to represent paint, also dribble some icing down the sides and dip the end of the brush into the icing. Attach the handle with royal icing and arrange the brush and lid as shown. With violet colouring, paint the wide brush strokes of paint on the board.

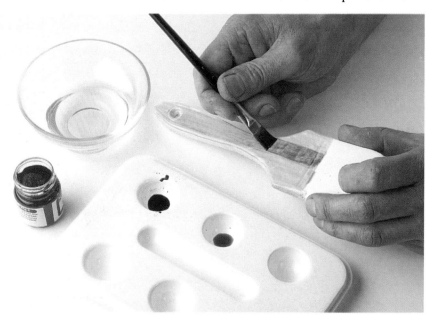

Paint the wood grain effect with brown colouring.

COMPUTER

Anyone with an interest in computers, whether for games or business, would be delighted with this realistic novelty cake.

CAKE

three 18cm (7inch) square Madeira cakes (page 6)
20cm (8inch) square Madeira cake (page 6)
500g (1lb/2 cups) buttercream (page 10)
140g (4½oz/scant ½ cup) jam for filling

DECORATION

2kg 125g (4lb 4oz) white sugarpaste
185g (6oz) pastillage (page 15)
paste food colourings – black, green
dusting powders (petal dust/blossom tint) – yellow, blue, red, cream
black food colour pen
liquorice
185g (6oz/1½ cups) royal icing (page 10)

EQUIPMENT

38cm (15inch) square cake board
cardboard tube
no. 1 and 3 piping tubes (tips)
foil
short length of wooden dowel
wooden skewer

1 Prepare in advance the modelled pencil holder, pencils, sheet of note paper and notepad, giving them time to dry adequately. Model each item from white pastillage, shaping the pencil holder around a cardboard tube to be removed later. The sheet of note paper is thinly rolled pastillage with a row of holes removed using tube (tip) no. 3, dried over crumpled foil.

Make the notepad from a thick rectangle of pastillage and punch out a row of holes. When dry, colour the items using dusting powders. The detail is added using a black food colour pen.

2 Prepare and layer the cakes (page 13), then cut and join as shown opposite. Cover the cakes completely with a thin spreading of buttercream.

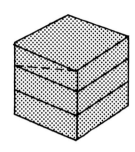

3 Roll out 750g (1lb 8oz) white sugarpaste and cover the board, using the method described on page 14.

4 Colour 125g (4oz) sugarpaste black and reserve. Using a small amount of black food colouring, colour the remaining sugarpaste grey. Roll out 185g (6oz) and cut into small squares as shown to make the keys. Allow to dry on a waxed paper lined tray.

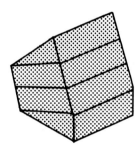

Computer

Cut out the keys from grey coloured sugarpaste.

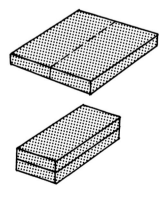

Keyboard build up

To personalize this cake, simply alter the inscription or message on the screen and also include the recipient's name. The date written on the notepad could be the birthday or anniversary of the individual.

5 Roll out the remaining grey sugarpaste and cover both cakes as described on page 14. Roll out the black sugarpaste thinly and cut out a rectangle for the screen, moisten the grey sugarpaste and attach the shape. Roll out some grey trimmings and cut into strips, moisten the edges of the black screen and attach the strips to create a frame.

6 Unravel the liquorice and wind neatly around a short length of waxed paper lined dowel. Place on a waxed paper lined tray and bake at 160°C (325°F/Gas 3) for about 6 minutes. Remove from the oven, cool slightly then carefully unwind from the dowel.

Shape liquorice around a piece of wooden dowel.

7 Colour 45g (1½oz/⅓ cup) royal icing black and, using tube (tip) no. 1, pipe the letters and numerals onto the prepared grey sugarpaste keys. Set aside to dry. Attach to the prepared keyboard cake with dabs of royal icing.

Pipe the letters and numbers with black icing.

8 Colour 45g (1½oz/⅓ cup) royal icing green and, using tube (tip) no. 1, pipe the inscription in 'digital' style lettering onto the black screen. See Hint for other inscription or message ideas.

HAPPY
BIRTHDAY

9 Position the screen cake and keyboard cake on to the prepared board and secure with dabs of the remaining royal icing. Make a small hole in the side of each cake using a wooden skewer. Link the two cakes together by inserting the prepared liquorice coil into the holes. Arrange the prepared pencil holder, pencils and notepad on the board, securing each with dabs of royal icing.

DESERT ISLAND

CAKE

two 15cm (6inch) round Madeira cakes (page 6)
185g (6oz/¾ cup) buttercream (page 10)
60g (2oz/scant ¼ cup) jam for filling

DECORATION

940g (1lb 14oz) white sugarpaste
220g (7oz) pastillage (page 15)
60g (2oz/¼ cup) caster (superfine) sugar
paste food colourings – paprika, green, yellow, brown,
red, tangerine, blueberry, blue, peach
dusting powders (petal dust/blossom tint) – orange,
brown
155g (5oz/1¼ cups) royal icing (page 10)
clear alcohol – gin or vodka

EQUIPMENT

30cm (12inch) round cake board
cocktail stick (toothpick)
curved former (page 15)
plastic or wooden dowel
no. 2 sable paint brush

HINT

To make this cake more suited to a sun worshipper or for a happy holiday cake, make a pastillage sunshine as described for the Greenhouse cake (page 72) and attach to the back of the board to peep over the island.

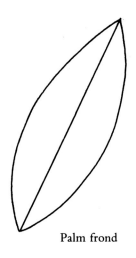

Palm frond

1   Colour the caster (superfine) sugar with paprika colouring to create the sand. Spread the coloured sugar on a greaseproof paper (parchment) lined tray and allow to dry naturally for use later.

2   Roll out thinly 60g (2oz) pastillage. Make a template of the design provided and cut out seven palm fronds. Use a cocktail stick (toothpick) as shown to frill the edges. Mark the vein detail using the back of a knife and cut a few slits. Allow the shapes to dry over a former as shown.

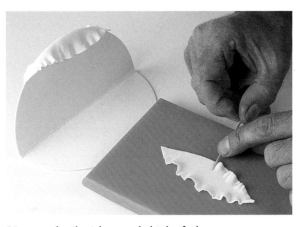

Use a cocktail stick to curl the leaf edges.

3   For the trunk of the palm tree, roll out 60g (2oz) mustard (yellow and brown) coloured pastillage and cut into strips. Wrap a strip around the dowel, moisten the end and secure. Repeat the method, overlapping each strip until the dowel is almost fully covered, leaving 7.5cm (3inch) exposed and allow to dry.

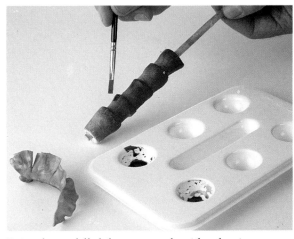

Paint the modelled dry tree trunk with colourings.

4   Make templates of the designs provided for the star fish, shells and leaping fish. Roll out the remaining pastillage and cut out the shapes. Allow the pieces to dry. Model the body of the crab and claws. Allow to dry, then join parts together with royal icing.

Mark the detail on the pastillage while still soft.

5   When all the prefabricated pieces are fully set, add the detail and effects using painting and dusting (page 19) techniques.

6   Colour 470g (15oz) sugarpaste blue. Use the basic method described on page 14 to cover the cake board, then refer to special effects (page 16) to create a sea effect.

7   Prepare and layer the cakes (page 13), then using a small serrated knife cut away small irregular shaped pieces from the top edge of the cake. Position the pieces around the cakes at random, attaching to the main cake with buttercream – this will create the basic island shape.

Alternatively, truffle paste (page 9) can be used to make the rugged island shape. Cover the cake completely with a thin spreading of buttercream.

8   Colour 470g (15oz) sugarpaste peach. Roll out the sugarpaste and cover the cake as described on page 14, pressing the sugarpaste gently into the contoured surface.

9   Brush the sugarpaste surface lightly with alcohol and sprinkle with the prepared coloured caster (superfine) sugar to create a sand effect. Remove excess sugar. Position the cake off-centre on the cake board, securing with a dab of royal icing.

10   Position the tree trunk into the cake, securing with a little royal icing – allow to set. Attach the leaves individually with royal icing, leaving each one to set before adding another. Position and attach the shells, star fish, crab and leaping fish as shown.

Sprinkle coloured caster sugar to create sand.

SLIMMER'S CAKE

This realistic bathroom scales cake is too good not to taste, even for the most weight conscious.

CAKE

20cm (8inch) square Madeira cake (page 6)
125g (4oz/½ cup) buttercream (page 10)
185g (6oz/½ cup) jam for filling

DECORATION

1kg 185g (2lb 6oz) white sugarpaste
125g (4oz) pastillage (page 15)
paste food colourings – black, pink, claret, violet
black food colour pen
60g (2oz/½ cup) royal icing (page 10)
silver colouring

EQUIPMENT

33cm (13inch) square cake board
no. 1 piping tube (tip)
ribbed rolling pin
paint brush

1 Prepare and layer the cake (page 13), then cut as shown opposite and shape each corner to a curve. Cover the cake completely with a thin spreading of buttercream.

2 Take 440g (14oz) sugarpaste and divide equally into two pieces. Colour one half of the sugarpaste black. Roll out and cut into 8.5cm (3½ inch) squares, cover with polythene to prevent crusting while the white paste is rolled and cut exactly the same. Moisten the cake board and arrange the prepared squares at an angle to represent a tiled floor. Neaten all joins and trim off the excess sugarpaste.

3 Make a template from the dial outline, roll out thinly a small piece of white pastillage and cut out the required shape. Colour 30g (1oz) pastillage pink, roll out very thinly and cut out the oblong plaque shape. Set both shapes aside to dry. Using a black food colour pen, draw on the dial markings. Make a tracing of a suitable inscription and transfer onto the prepared plaque. Pipe the lettering using tube (tip) no. 1 with black royal icing.

Use a food colour pen to draw detail on scale dial.

4 Colour 500g (1lb) of the remaining sugarpaste pale lilac using claret and violet food colouring and 250g (8oz) grey using black food colouring. Roll out the lilac sugarpaste and texture it using the ribbed rolling pin. Use to cover the cake as described on page 14. Roll out the grey coloured sugarpaste and again texture it. Cut into long narrow strips the same depth as the cake side. Moisten the sides of the covered cake and

HINT

To ensure you create an authentic effect, it is a good idea to have a real tape measure to hand from which to copy the detail.

To make painting the dial easier, prepare it off the cake to be attached with royal icing.

Allow sugarpaste to dry before painting on detail.

Have a real tape measure to hand to copy from.

attach the strips, gently pressing into place without distorting the ribbed pattern.

5   Place the previously prepared template of the dial design onto the sugarpaste covering. Cut around the shape and remove the portion to be replaced with the prepared dial. Edge the dial with a thin strip of lilac coloured sugarpaste.

6   Roll out the white pastillage into a long narrow piece and cut into a neat strip 30mm (1¼inches) wide for the tape measure. Attach the strip to the cake with dabs of royal icing, arranging with random curves and forming a tied knot effect at the front of the scales. Allow to dry completely.

7   Using a black food colour pen, draw the measurement markings and numbers on the tape measure. Paint the 'metal' tape measure ends using a paint brush with silver colouring. Attach the prepared inscription plaque, securing with a dab of royal icing.

Dial

SEWING BOX

As a personal touch, pipe in stitch effect a suitable inscription and the name on this beautiful life-like cake.

CAKE
20 × 15cm (8 × 6inch) oval Madeira cake (page 6)
250g (8oz/1cup) buttercream (page 10)
75g (2½oz/¼ cup) jam for filling
DECORATION
1kg (2lb) white sugarpaste
90g (3oz) pastillage (page 15)
625g (1lb 4oz) marzipan (almond paste)
500g (1lb/4 cups) royal icing (page 10)
paste food colourings – chestnut, claret, pink, violet, black – plus a selection of colours for buttons and material
confectioner's varnish
silver colouring
EQUIPMENT
35 × 30cm (14 × 12inch) oval cake board
ribbed rolling pin
round cutters
no. 1, 2, 3, 13, 22 and 43 piping tubes (tips)
crimper
straight frill cutter (optional)

HINT

With the many sugarcraft methods available to emulate various needlework techniques, you may like to introduce edible sugarpaste material featuring appliqué, smocking and cross-stitch to make the cake even more interesting.

1 Roll into a sausage shape 220g (7oz) white sugarpaste to make the cotton reel centres. Colour 60g (2oz) pale chestnut for the cotton reel tops, then divide and colour the remainder for the cotton colours. Roll out and form as shown using a ribbed rolling pin to create the thread effect. Join all parts by moistening with water. A lose thread can be piped using tube (tip) no. 1 with royal icing.

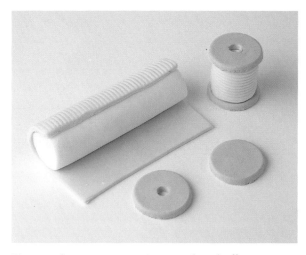

Texture the sugarpaste to create a thread effect.

2 Roll out some various colours of sugarpaste and use different sized round cutters to make buttons. Use tubes (tips) no. 1 and 2 to make holes in the buttons. Allow to dry, then glaze with confectioner's varnish.

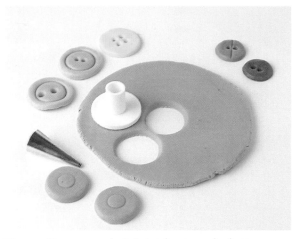

Use small cutters and piping tubes to make buttons.

3 Use the pastillage to model a small pair of scissors; have a real pair to hand to copy the proportions and shapes. Allow to dry, then paint with silver and pale chestnut colouring.

4 Prepare and layer the cake (page 13). Cover the cake completely with a thin spreading of buttercream.

5 Roll out the marzipan (almond paste) and cover the cake as described for sugarpaste on page 14. Place the cake on a waxed paper lined workboard ready to decorate.

6 Colour 250g (8oz/2cups) of the royal icing dark claret and use 100g (3½oz/scant 1 cup) to fill a piping bag fitted with tube (tip) no. 3 inserted. Cover the remaining dark claret icing with a moist cloth and set aside for use later. Colour the remaining icing light claret and use some to fill a piping bag fitted with a basketweave tube no. 22. Pipe the basketweave onto the cake side as shown in the technique photograph here. Refer to the illustrations and method opposite.

Practise piping the basketweave technique on card.

Using the no. 3 tube (tip), pipe a vertical line. With the basketweave tube, pipe short horizontal bands. The distance between each band should be the width of the basketweave tube. Ensure the bands are all the same length.

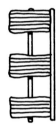

Pipe a second vertical line just resting on the edge of the bands.

Again pipe short horizontal bands, this time between the first piped ones. Repeat the technique to complete the basketweave.

7 Make a template of the oval lid shape and cover with waxed paper on a flat board. Pipe the basketweave as described. Allow to dry, then edge with a line piped using tube (tip) no. 43 with the reserved dark claret icing. Pipe a small curved handle onto waxed paper using tube (tip) no. 13 with dark claret icing. When dry, attach to the lid.

8 Take 500g (1lb) sugarpaste and colour half violet and half pink. Roll out the pink and violet paste separately and cut into narrow strips. Moisten the cake board with water and lay alternate coloured strips to cover the board. Trim off the excess sugarpaste and crimp the edge.

9 Remove the prepared cake from the waxed paper and position on the prepared board, securing with a dab of icing. Pipe a small line border around the top and base edge using tube (tip) no. 43 with dark claret icing – allow to dry.

10 Roll out two colours of the remaining sugarpaste very thinly and cut into squares for the material. Fancy edges can be created using a straight frill cutter. Arrange the material pieces quickly into folds and drapes before they set, tucking some inside and resting some on top of the prepared lid. Attach the lid and pieces with dabs of icing.

Arrange the sugarpaste material squares on the box lid and pipe the needles and thread last.

11 Arrange and attach the prepared cotton reels, buttons and scissors with dabs of icing. Make the needles by piping onto waxed paper using tube (tip) no. 1 with white icing. Allow to dry, then paint with silver colouring. Attach the needles with dabs of icing and pipe thread using tube (tip) no. 1 with black royal icing.

CAN OF BEER

CAKE
25 × 10cm (10 × 4inch) Swiss roll (page 8)
155g (5oz/⅔ cup) buttercream (page 10)
DECORATION
1kg 375g (2lb 12oz) white sugarpaste
155g (5oz) pastillage (page 15)
paste food colourings – black, red
gold and silver colouring
90g (3oz/¾ cup) royal icing (page 10)
EQUIPMENT
25cm (10inch) square cake board
large oval cutter
former
no. 3 and 8 sable paint brushes
oiled parchment or thin card
no. 1 piping tube (tip)

HINT

The can design featured here is just an example, find out the recipient's favourite tipple and copy the design. Copying can designs for personal use is normally acceptable, but for commercial use you must obtain the permission from the copyright owner.

1 For the can label, roll out the pastillage and cut out using a large oval cutter. Roll a tube of card to the same curve as the Swiss roll and secure with tape to make a former. Line with waxed paper and place the shape on. Allow to dry completely, then paint with gold colouring.

2 Stand the Swiss roll on end and cover with a thin spreading of buttercream. Colour 875g (1lb 12oz) sugarpaste black and use to cover the cake as described on page 14. Using the oval

cutter, cut out a section of black sugarpaste from the covered cake and replace with the prepared oval gold label. Paint a line of gold around the label edge. Model the rim and ring pull from sugarpaste, moisten and attach to the cake. Allow to dry, then paint with silver colouring.

When dry, paint the oval shape with gold colouring.

3 Into the remaining white sugarpaste, mix a few black sugarpaste trimmings – don't mix through completely. Roll out the paste to create a marbled effect (page 16). Cover the board with the prepared sugarpaste as described on page 14.

4 Trace the beer name lettering, then using a craft knife, cut out from parchment. Colour 60g (2oz) royal icing black and stencil the name on the label. Use tube (tip) no. 1 with black icing and then the same tube with the remaining icing coloured red to pipe the lettering. Secure the cake to the prepared board with icing.

GUINNESS

'GUINNESS' and the harp device are registered trade marks for beer.

PIANO

For added detail, decorate the top of the piano with a moulded sugarpaste candelabra or a vase of flowers. A modelled piano stool could be included too.

CAKE
20cm (8inch) square Madeira cake (page 6)
125g (4oz/½ cup) buttercream (page 10)
90g (3oz/¼ cup) jam for filling
DECORATION
1kg 250g (2lb 8oz) white sugarpaste
90g (3oz) pastillage (page 15)
paste food colourings – brown, chestnut, orange, black
orange dusting powder (petal dust/blossom tint)
black food colour pen
10cm (4inch) square rice (wafer) paper
90g (3oz/¾ cup) royal icing (page 10)
confectioner's varnish
EQUIPMENT
30cm (12inch) square cake board
ribbed rolling pin
no. 2 piping tube (tip)
small piece of polystyrene

1 Colour the pastillage with brown and chestnut and roll out. Cut out the keyboard base rectangle and ends, piano legs and music sheet holder – allow to dry. Make a tracing from the design provided overleaf and cut out the music sheet from rice (wafer) paper. Use a black food colour pen to draw on the detail, which may be original music, the recipient's favourite tune or a suitable inscription.

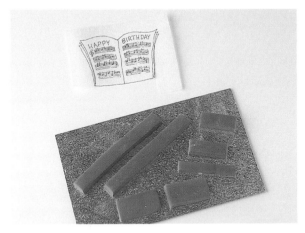

Prepare the music sheet and cut out pieces.

2 Colour 440g (14oz) sugarpaste orange and roll out. Texture the sugarpaste using a ribbed rolling pin, then cover the board using the method described on page 14. To make the board more attractive, use orange dusting powder to tint at random.

3 Prepare and layer the cake (page 13). Stand the cake on end and cover completely with a thin spreading of buttercream. Reserve 75g (2½oz) white sugarpaste and colour the remainder using brown and chestnut colouring to match pastillage. Roll out the brown sugarpaste and cover the cake as described on page 14.

4 Roll out the brown sugarpaste trimmings and cut into long narrow strips. Take time to make neat corners, cutting the strips at angles to create a mitred effect. Attach to the cake by moistening with water.

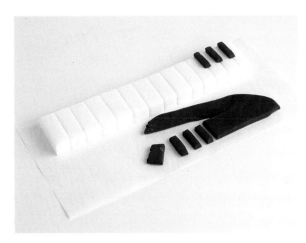

Neatly cut out the white and black piano keys.

Support the attached keyboard until completely dry.

5 Roll out the remaining white sugarpaste and cut out a long narrow strip as shown. Mark the keys using the back of a knife. Colour the sugarpaste trimmings black, roll out and cut the keys. Attach to the white keys by moistening with water.

6 Colour 45g (1½oz) royal icing brown and fill a small piping bag fitted with tube (tip) no. 2. Set aside to use for attaching and joining the prepared parts. Position the cake on the prepared board and secure with the remaining icing. Attach the keyboard base to the cake with the brown icing, support the base with blocks of polystyrene. Attach the keyboard, keyboard ends, music holder and finally the legs. Continue supporting until all the joins are completely dry. Glaze all the brown sugarpaste and pastillage with confectioner's varnish. Allow to dry, then place the prepared music sheet on.

Music sheet

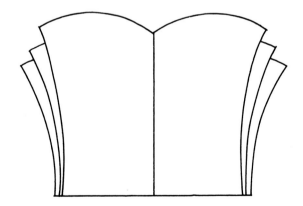

TOY BOX

A child's dream – this cake will enthral children of all ages. Model the child's favourite toys to surround the toy box.

CAKE
three 15cm (6inch) square Madeira cakes (page 6)
280g (9oz/generous 1 cup) buttercream (page 10)
75g (2½oz/¼ cup) jam for filling
DECORATION
1kg 500g (3lb) white sugarpaste
about 1kg (2lb) sugarpaste – assorted colours
paste food colourings – blue, red, yellow, black
about 125g (4oz/1cup) royal icing (page 10)
EQUIPMENT
36cm (14inch) square cake board
flower cutter
petal or leaf cutter
oiled parchment or thin card
craft knife
no. 1 and 2 piping tubes (tips)

1 Colour 60g (2oz) sugarpaste blue and 60g (2oz) red, set aside. Colour 625g (1lb 4oz) sugarpaste bright yellow. Make a template to the size of one cake top, about a 15cm (6inch) square. Roll out the yellow sugarpaste and cut out five squares. Lay the squares carefully onto a waxed paper lined flat tray or board. While the sugarpaste is still soft, use the flower and petal cutters to remove a pattern from the centre of four of the squares. Roll out the red and blue sugarpaste. Using the same cutters, inlay shapes in the yellow sugarpaste squares, smoothing gently with the fingers to conceal the joins.

Use inlay techniques to create a colourful pattern.

2 Make a tracing of the word 'TOYS' (overleaf) for the lid and transfer onto parchment. Using a sharp craft knife, cut out the letters to make a stencil. Colour 30g (1oz) royal icing red and, using a palette knife, stencil the wording onto the undecorated yellow paste square.

Cut out a lettering stencil for the toy box lid.

HINT

It is useful when making the edible toys to have at hand a child's nursery or colouring book from which to glean inspiration and also to provide you with proportions of size and colour ideas.

Roll out the yellow sugarpaste trimmings and cut into long narrow strips. Moisten the edges of the lid and attach the strips, using a small knife to cut neat mitred corners. Allow to dry.

Prepare and layer the cakes (page 13), one on top of the other to make a cube shape, ensuring that all sides are equal. Trim if necessary. Cover the cake completely with a thin spreading of buttercream.

Colour 750g (1lb 8oz) sugarpaste black and roll out 125g (4oz), cut out a square to the size of the cake top and attach – the buttercream will secure it in place. Roll out the remaining black sugarpaste and cover the board, using the method described on page 14.

Carefully remove the prepared toy box sides and attach them to the cake, securing them to the buttercream. Conceal the joins with strips of yellow sugarpaste. Attach the prepared toy box lid with a dab of royal icing.

Each individual child for which you make this attractive novelty will no doubt have their own favourite toys to be copied and featured on the cake. Edible toys are quite simple to make from various colours of sugarpaste – rolled, textured, modelled and joined. Eyes and features can be piped on using royal icing. Rather than make the toys and letting them dry, make each one and position on the cake, securing with royal icing; in this way you can make them look as if they have been casually dropped around the box and on top of each other.

Position prepared cake on the covered cake board.

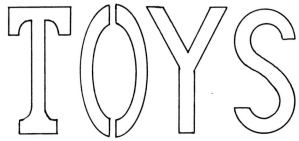

GARDENER'S DELIGHT

The small seedling plant in the pot could be replaced with a larger sugar modelled flower or foliage plant. Alternatively to save time, use some good quality silk or fabric blooms.

HINT

Depending on the time available, more detail could be included by using a clay gun to make the grass and soil effect as described on pages 16 and 18.

CAKE
15cm (6inch) square Madeira cake (page 6)
½ length Swiss roll (page 8)
220g (7oz/⅞ cup) buttercream (page 10)
90g (3oz/¼ cup) jam for filling
DECORATION
1kg 560g (3lb 2oz) white sugarpaste
500g (1lb) pastillage (page 15)
paste food colourings – yellow, brown, blue, green, peach, paprika, black
dusting powders (petal dust/blossom tint) – orange, brown, green
food colour pens – brown, black
silver colouring
155g (5oz/1¼ cups) royal icing (page 10)
EQUIPMENT
38cm (15inch) square cake board
small cake board
formers
no. 1 and 3 sable paint brushes
foil
leaf cutter
dog bone modelling tool

1 Colour 315g (10oz) pastillage for the seed box using yellow and brown food colouring. Roll out thinly and cut out two rectangles 23 × 6cm (9 × 2½ inches) and two 15 × 6cm (6 × 2½ inches). Place onto a waxed paper lined flat tray or board to dry, also model four corner pieces. When dry, use orange and brown dusting powders and a brown food colour pen to create a wood grain effect as described on page 18.

2 Roll out the remaining coloured pastillage and model two handles for the garden tools. Allow to dry. When dry, colour with orange and brown dusting powder. Draw an outline from a real fork and trowel, then make a card template. Roll out 140g (4½oz) white pastillage and cut out the fork and trowel shapes. Make two formers from thick card, one curved and one vee shaped. Line with waxed paper and place the fork and trowel respectively into the formers. Allow to dry, then paint with silver colouring. Join the parts of the fork and trowel together with icing and support with crumpled foil until completely dry.

Use templates and formers to make the garden tools.

Roll out thinly 125g (4oz) white sugarpaste, cut out and model two seed packets (opposite). Allow to dry, then use a fine paint brush and food colourings to paint the packet design – refer to a real seed packet for ideas.

Paint the seed packet design using colourings.

Colour 45g (1½oz) pastillage pale green. Roll out the paste and, using a leaf cutter, cut out several shapes. Place the shapes individually in the palm of your hand and use a dog bone modelling tool to frill the edges. Allow the leaves to dry on crumpled foil. When dry, colour with green, orange and brown dusting powders.

Use a sharp serrated knife to cut and shape the Swiss roll into a plant pot shape. Cover the cake completely with a thin spreading of buttercream. Place the cake upside down onto a small cake board. Colour 375g (12oz) sugarpaste terracotta using peach and paprika food colouring. Roll out the sugarpaste and cover the cake and board as described on page 14. Cut out a long narrow strip of terracotta sugarpaste and attach to the base (the top when upturned) by moistening with water. Allow to dry. Turn the cake the right way up and carefully remove the cake board to leave a rim on the plant pot.

Dry leaves in crumpled foil for a natural effect.

Make a rim around the top of the plant pot cake.

Prepare the cake (page 13), then cut and layer as shown opposite. Cover the cake with a thin spreading of buttercream. Colour 185g (6oz) sugarpaste dark brown and roll out. Cut into a 23 × 15cm (9 × 6inch) rectangle and place on the prepared cake, the buttercream will secure it. Make indentations on the surface using fingers. Attach the prepared seed box sides and corners, joining with dabs of royal icing.

Colour 875g (1lb 12oz) sugarpaste green. Roll out and cover the board, using the method described on page 14. Place the prepared seed box and plant pot on the board, then arrange the seed packets and garden tools. When a pleasing layout has been achieved, secure all items with dabs of royal icing. Make holes in the brown sugarpaste soil and insert pairs of leaves. For the plant pot soil, colour 75g (2½oz) royal icing brown and spread onto the cake, insert a group of prepared leaves. Colour some sugarpaste trimmings black

and roll some tiny seeds to be sprinkled around the seed packets. Moisten with water to secure.

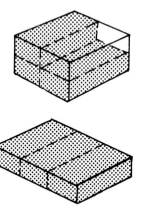

Attach the seed box sides to the prepared cake.

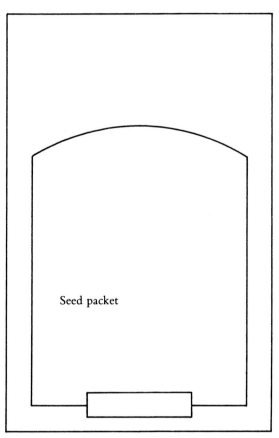

Seed packet

TRAINING SHOES

This pair of trendy training shoes would delight a sportsperson or jogger of any age! Of course, the colour of the trainers can be altered to match the favourite pair belonging to the recipient.

CAKE

20cm (8inch) square chocolate Madeira cake (page 6)
500g (1lb/2 cups) chocolate buttercream (page 10)
1 chocolate Swiss roll (page 8)
1 recipe truffle paste (page 9)
90g (3oz/¼ cup) jam for filling

DECORATION

1.5kg (3lb) white sugarpaste
470g (15oz/3¾ cups) royal icing (page 10)
paste food colourings – green, blue, black, red, yellow
gold colouring

EQUIPMENT

35cm (14inch) hexagonal cake board
ribbed rolling pin
no. 1, 2 and 4 piping tubes (tips)
no. 1 sable paint brush
cheese grater

Make a template of the shoe design (overleaf) provided and place on one half of the 20cm (8inch) square cake, cut out a left shoe shape. Turn the template over and cut out a matching right shoe. Prepare and layer the cakes as described on page 13.

Cut the Swiss roll into two 7.5cm (3inch) lengths. Position and attach the pieces to the shoe shaped cakes with buttercream as shown above.

Model the shoe upper from prepared truffle paste.

Divide the truffle paste into two equal amounts and shape to form the rounded uppers of the shoes (these are easier to prepare on a work surface). Transfer the shapes onto the cakes and attach with buttercream. Cover the cakes completely with a thin spreading of chocolate buttercream.

Set aside 75g (2½oz/⅔ cup) royal icing for piping later. Colour the remaining icing green and cover the board to create a grass effect, using the method described on page 18.

Roll out 500g (1lb) white sugarpaste and cover one shoe cake, using the method described on page 14. Drape the sugarpaste loosely over the cake and, because of the unusual shape, use the palm of your hand rather than a

Shoe sole

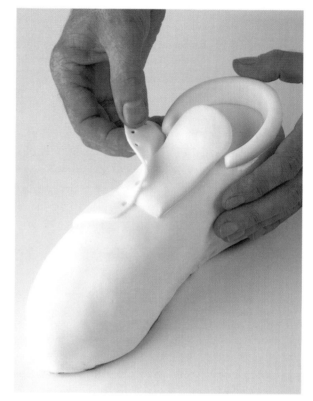

Carefully position and attach the shoe detail.

cake smoother to create a neat finish. Repeat the same procedure for the other shoe. Use some of the trimmings to shape the padded top for the opening of each shoe, attaching by moistening with water.

6 Roll out the remaining sugarpaste thickly and cut out the two shapes required for each shoe to form the lace sections. To make the chunky soles of the shoes, roll out the sugarpaste thinly and texture using a ribbed rolling pin. Cut into narrow strips. Attach all the prepared pieces to the shoes by moistening lightly with a little water

brushed on. Smooth the joins with the fingers where necessary. (Roll, cut out and attach each of the pieces described separately, otherwise the sugarpaste may crust before you have time to work it.)

7 While the paste is still soft, use the back of a small knife to make indentations and markings to represent joins as shown. Remove a line of lace holes from the sugarpaste using piping tube (tip) no. 4. Also remove a pattern of air holes on the uppers using tube (tip) no. 2. Paint the shoe lining with blue colour thickened with a little royal icing. Paint the flash with blue colouring.

8 Using half of the reserved royal icing, pipe the lace eyelets on using tube (tip) no. 2. Allow to dry, then paint with gold colouring. Use black colouring to colour the remaining icing grey and, using tube (tip) no. 1, pipe on the stitching detail.

Apply the stitching using a fine piping tube (tip).

9 The 'designer' motif of your choice is painted (page 19) directly onto the shoe using a no. 1 paint brush with colourings. Alternatively, prepare on a piece of sugarpaste and attach to the shoe. Paint on any other colour details.

10 The laces can be real shoe laces, cut in half and tipped with flower tape to seal the frayed edge before inserting them into the sugarpaste. Alternatively, roll out strips of sugarpaste and mark with the small pattern of a cheese grater to create a textured effect.

Use a fine paint brush to add detailed colour work.

BEST BUBBLY

What better way to celebrate than with champagne – both cake and the liquid kind! The instructions here could easily be adapted to make a bottle of wine, spirit or favourite tipple.

CAKE
15 × 7.5cm (6 × 3inch) Swiss roll (page 8)
100g (3½oz/½ cup) buttercream (page 10)
DECORATION
750g (1lb 8oz) white sugarpaste
375g (12oz) pastillage (page 15)
155g (5oz/1¼ cups) royal icing (page 10)
paste food colourings – chestnut, green, peach
food colour pens – brown, black, green, yellow
white fat for greasing
silver and gold colouring
EQUIPMENT
25cm (10inch) round gold cake board
1 empty champagne bottle
no. 2 piping tube (tip)
six 28g flower wires, cut into various lengths
no. 1 sable paint brush
crimper
posy pick

HINT

Rather than leave the pastillage modelled neck of the bottle hollow, you could easily fill it with liqueur flavoured truffle paste (page 9), after joining and before attaching to the base cake.

Use the real champagne bottle neck label as a template outline.

WARNING

Remember to remove the bubble wires before eating the cake.

1 Wash and dry the champagne bottle and lightly grease the neck. Roll out the pastillage and carefully wrap around the neck of the bottle as shown. Trim with a knife and smooth neatly. While still soft, carefully cut through the paste down the length on both sides. Allow to dry completely. When dry, carefully remove the two halves from the bottle. If the pastillage is difficult to remove, gently warm using the heat

Cover the bottle neck with sugarpaste and trim.

Cut a separating line ready for easy removal.

from an angled desk lamp to aid easy release. Join together using tube (tip) no. 2 with white royal icing.

2 Use half of the pastillage trimmings coloured pale chestnut to model a cork as shown. When dry, paint and draw the detail on using colourings and a brown food colour pen. Also paint the top with silver colouring.

Model the cork and paint detail with colourings.

Paint the wired bubbles with silver colouring.

3 To make bubbles, roll the remaining pastillage into various sized small balls. Attach each ball onto flower wire and insert into polystyrene to dry. When dry, paint the balls and wire with silver colouring.

4 Stand the Swiss roll on end and cover completely with a thin spreading of buttercream. Roll out 440g (14oz) white sugarpaste and cover the cake, using the method described on page 14. Attach the prepared bottle top with icing. Roll out some paste trimmings very thinly and cut out a 10cm (4inch) square. Moisten the bottle neck and wrap the square around, leaving the top uneven. When dry, paint the bottle with green food colouring and the icing foil with gold.

Make a template of the neck label and cut out from thinly rolled sugarpaste trimmings. Also cut out a square label. Attach to the bottle by moistening with water – allow to dry. Paint and draw the label designs on using colourings and food colour pens.

5 Colour 250g (8oz) sugarpaste pale peach. Roll out and cut out a 15cm (6inch) circle, crimp the edge. Moisten the board with a little water and place the prepared circle on. Position the cake and secure with a dab of icing. Attach the cork with water. Roll out the remaining sugarpaste very thinly and cut out a 15cm (6inch) square. Fold the paste and drape near the bottle to represent a napkin. Carefully insert a posy pick into the top of the bottle, securing with a little icing. Pipe some icing into the posy pick and insert the prepared bubbles at various heights.

TULIP BOUQUET

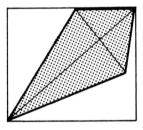

The delicate flowers which adorn this beautiful cake are made from rice paper.

CAKE

28cm (11inch) square Madeira cake (page 6)
410g (13oz/1⅔ cups) buttercream (page 10)
185g (6oz/¼ cup) jam for filling

DECORATION

1kg 875g (3lb 12oz) white sugarpaste
paste food colourings – blue, green black, pink
dusting powders (petal dust/blossom tint) – pink, red, orange, green, yellow
90g (3oz/¾ cup) royal icing (page 10)
four A4 sheets rice paper
black food colour pen

EQUIPMENT

35 × 30cm (14 × 12inch) oblong cake board, cut into diamond shape as shown
cotton wool or foil
plaque cutter
no. 1 and 3 piping tubes (tips)
5mm (¼inch) chisel head sable paint brush
10cm (4inches) fine gold thread

1 Cut the cake in half to make two oblong shapes 28 × 14cm (11 × 5½inches). Prepare and layer both pieces (page 13) to make a double depth cake. Using a sharp knife, carve the cake to form a bottle neck shape as shown. Cover the cake completely with buttercream.

2 Colour 500g (1lb) sugarpaste deep blue and cover the board, using the method described on page 14.

3 Roll out 1kg 250g (2lb 8oz) white sugarpaste to a 35cm (14inch) square, place the cake on aligning point-to-point. Wrap the sugarpaste around the cake as for a bunch of real flowers, bringing the left side over first, then the right side. Support any overlapping sugarpaste with cotton wool or crumpled foil until dry.

Spread the prepared cake shape with buttercream.

Wrap the sugarpaste neatly around the cake.

Cake board

HINT

Create your own individual bouquet by making different flowers and leaves, or use good quality silk flower heads. You could also leave the wrapping paper a plain colour or change the stripes to a different pattern.

Cut out a pastillage plaque – colour when dry.

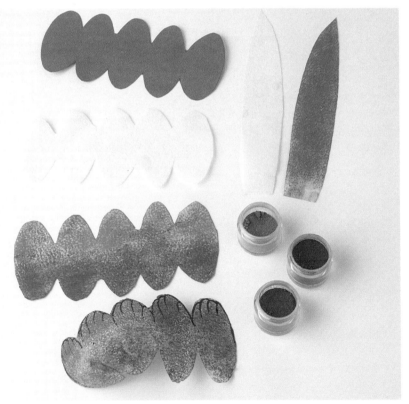

Make the petals and leaves from rice (wafer) paper.

4 Colour 60g (2oz) sugarpaste green and roll out into thick stem shapes. Cut into various lengths and set aside to dry.

5 Roll out thinly the remaining sugarpaste and make a gift tag using a plaque cutter. Make a small hole using tube (tip) no. 3. Allow the plaque to dry, then tint the edges with pink dusting powder. Make a tracing of the lettering on page 80 and transfer onto the plaque. Pipe using tube (tip) no. 1 with black royal icing.

6 Make templates from the designs on page 80 and cut out seven tulip petal shapes and several leaves from the rice paper. Prepare colours by adding a little icing (confectioner's) sugar to some dusting powders, blending with your fingers. Put some of the blended powder on to the right (smooth) side of the rice paper and rub it in gently, following the grain of the paper. Colour the petals orange and red, and the leaves green with a touch of yellow. Shake off the excess colour. Draw outlines and detail on the petals using a black food colour pen. Curl the petals as shown and secure by lightly moistening the rice paper with water.

7 Mix a small amount of pink colour with water and, using a chisel head brush, paint the stripes on the wrapping paper – allow to dry. Transfer the cake onto the prepared board, securing with a dab of royal icing. Attach the leaves and tulip heads with small dabs of icing and insert the stems to the other end of the cake. Position and attach the gift tag with icing and finish by threading and looping fine gold thread through the gift tag.

GREENHOUSE

To create a realistic glass effect, cut out shapes of leaf gelatine to fit the various greenhouse panes (see page 16).

CAKE
three 20cm (8inch) square Madeira cakes (page 6)
470g (15oz/2 cups) buttercream (page 10)
315g (10oz/1 cup) jam for filling
DECORATION
2kg 375g (4lb 12oz) white sugarpaste
90g (3oz) pastillage (page 15)
paste food colourings – yellow, blue, paprika, peach, red, violet, orange, brown, green
dusting powders (petal dust/blossom tint) – yellow, orange, red
food colour pens – orange, black
200g (7oz/1¾ cups) royal icing (page 10)
EQUIPMENT
33cm (13inch) square cake board
petal cutter
small round cutter
scriber
no. 1 and 2 sable paint brushes
brickwork rolling pin (page 16)
small piece of foam sponge for stippling
no. 2 piping tube (tip)

1 Make the templates of the sunshine design provided overleaf. Reserve 7g (¼oz) white pastillage and colour the remainder yellow. Roll out the pastillage thinly and cut the three-quarter circle and petal shapes. Lay the circle onto a waxed paper lined board, moisten the edges and attach the petal shapes.

2 Using a small round cutter, remove two holes for the eyes. Roll out the white pastillage and cut out two circles to fill the holes. Smooth with the fingers to conceal the join – allow to dry. When dry, colour with yellow and orange dusting powders. Use orange and black food colour pens to draw the nose, eyes and mouth.

Use a template and cutters to make the sunshine.

Use dusting techniques and food colour pens.

HINT

A door and roof window could be made in advance from pastillage and allowed to dry on waxed paper. The prepared pieces would then be attached to the cake with royal icing to appear as if they were ajar.

  If you do not have a brickwork rolling pin, a similar effect can be created using a small knife or by cutting out rectangles of sugarpaste (page 16).

Sunshine

Window detail

3 Prepare the cakes, cutting and shaping as shown opposite to form the basic house shape. Layer the cakes as described on page 13. Cover the cake completely with a thin spreading of buttercream.

4 Reserve 1kg 60g (2lb 2oz) sugarpaste for later use. Colour 45g (1½oz) sugarpaste blue and knead through the remaining white sugarpaste, do not mix thoroughly. Roll out to create a streaked appearance and cover the cake as described on page 14. Take care with the corners, smoothing with the fingers to create neat joins. The streaked effect will help convey the effect of glass in the finished greenhouse (see also the introduction to this recipe).

Cover the basic shape with blue tinted sugarpaste.

5 Use a ruler and scriber to mark the positions of the frame on the greenhouse. Make templates of the flower designs provided and, using a scriber, pin-prick onto the cake. Paint the flowers, foliage, seed boxes and plant pots using fine paint brushes with colourings and food colour pens – allow to dry.

6 Colour 280g (9oz) of the reserved sugarpaste with paprika and peach colouring. Roll out the sugarpaste and texture with a brickwork rolling pin. Cut the prepared paste into the required shapes, moisten the lower half of the cake and attach the shapes to make the wall. Leave a gap for the door. Allow to dry, then tint with orange and red dusting powders.

7 Colour 155g (5oz) of the reserved sugarpaste brown for the frame. Roll out and cut into long narrow strips. Attach to the cake by moistening with water, using the pre-marked lines as a guide.

8 Colour the remaining sugarpaste green and cover the board, using the method described on page 14. Colour 60g (2oz) royal icing green and, using a small piece of foam sponge, stipple the board to create a grass effect. Allow to dry, then place the cake onto the board and secure with dabs of icing. Using sugarpaste trimmings, make a path following the method for cobbles described on page 16. Attach the prepared pastillage sunshine with a line of royal icing piped using tube (tip) no. 2.

Outline flowers and pots with a food colour pen.

Attach strips of brown sugarpaste for the frame.

BIG SPENDER

A glaze of confectioner's varnish will add a leather-look sheen to this larger-than-life wallet full of money and credit cards!

CAKE
20cm (8inch) square Madeira cake (page 6)
410g (13oz/1⅔ cups) buttercream (page 10)
155g (5oz/½ cup) jam for filling

DECORATION
1kg 660g (3lb 6oz) white sugarpaste
375g (12oz) pastillage (page 15)
silver and gold colouring
paste food colourings – peach, orange, brown, black, green, red, yellow, pink
food colour pens – green, violet, brown, black
125g (4oz/1cup) royal icing (page 10)

EQUIPMENT
38 × 30cm (15 × 12inch) oblong cake board
foil
small round cutters
no. 1 and 2 sable paint brushes

1 Make templates for the credit cards and paper money. Roll out the pastillage thinly and cut out the required number of shapes. Place the credit card shapes onto a waxed paper lined flat tray or board to dry. The paper money shapes are dried on crumpled foil to create a used effect. Also make a few narrow paper money tops to insert into the wallet. Roll out remaining pastillage thickly and cut out various sized rounds for coins.

2 When dry, paint the coins with silver and gold colouring. Paint the detail on the paper

Prepare the modelled pastillage money and coins.

Paint detail using colourings and food colour pens.

money using paint brushes with colourings as described on page 19. Use food colour pens to draw lines, lettering and borders.

3 Paint the designs on the credit cards as described previously for the paper money. You can create your own unique credit card designs or adapt the images from real ones.

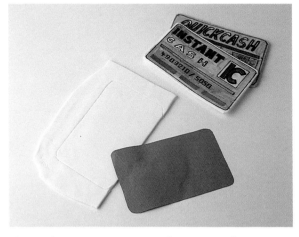

A template ensures accuracy when cutting shapes.

4 Divide the cake into two pieces, cutting horizontally through the middle as described on page 13. Layer and position upright as shown, joining with jam. Cover the cakes completely with a thin spreading of buttercream.

5 Colour 875g (1lb 12oz) sugarpaste brown. Roll out and cover the cakes using the method described on page 14. Re-roll the trimmings and cut out strips, attach to both sides of the cake with water to make pockets. Make a large square for the left side, attaching the same. Model a fastener and attach with water.

6 Colour 685g (1lb 6oz) sugarpaste peach and cover the board, using the method described on page 14. Colour the remaining sugarpaste deep peach and roll into a long rope, also roll the pale peach sugarpaste trimmings the same. Twist the two rolls together and gently and carefully re-roll. Moisten the edges of the covered board and attach the prepared sugarpaste twist to make a decorative edging.

7 Position the cake onto the board and secure with dabs of royal icing. The paper money tops are attached to the wallet with a piped line of royal icing. Arrange the paper money, credit cards and coins casually in and around the wallet as shown, securing with dabs of royal icing.

HINT

To create a different effect use the method described on page 16 to make marbling, use the mottled sugarpaste to cover the wallet.

To make a template for the credit cards, increase the outline in proportion of a real credit card.

Prepare and position the cake ready to decorate.

At this stage, glaze the wallet if required.

78

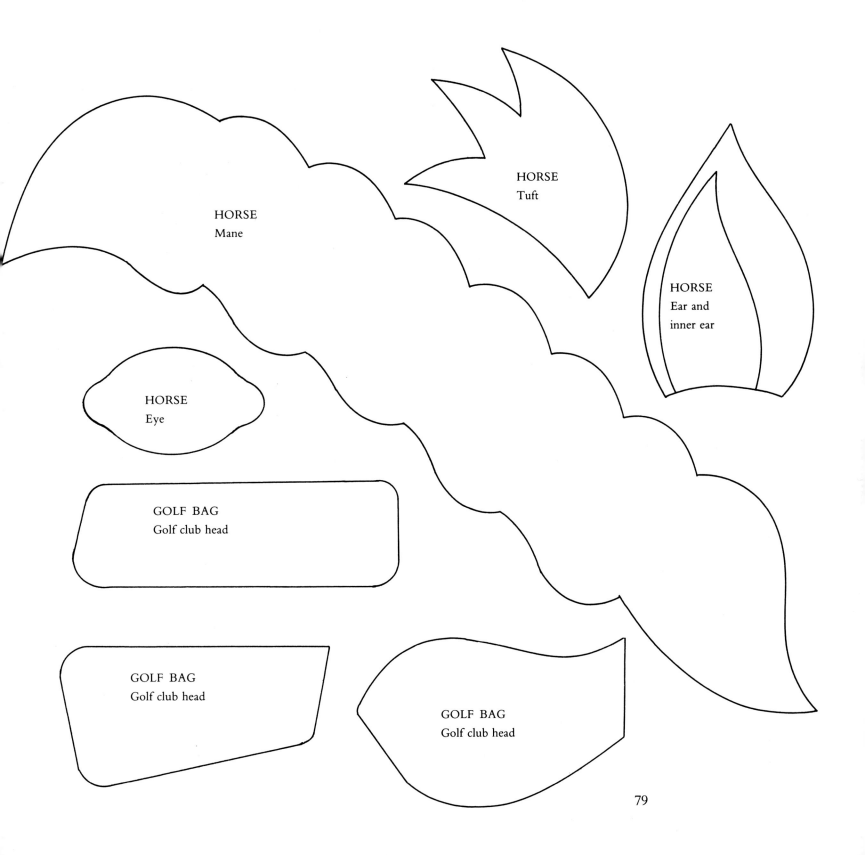

HORSE
Mane

HORSE
Tuft

HORSE
Ear and
inner ear

HORSE
Eye

GOLF BAG
Golf club head

GOLF BAG
Golf club head

GOLF BAG
Golf club head

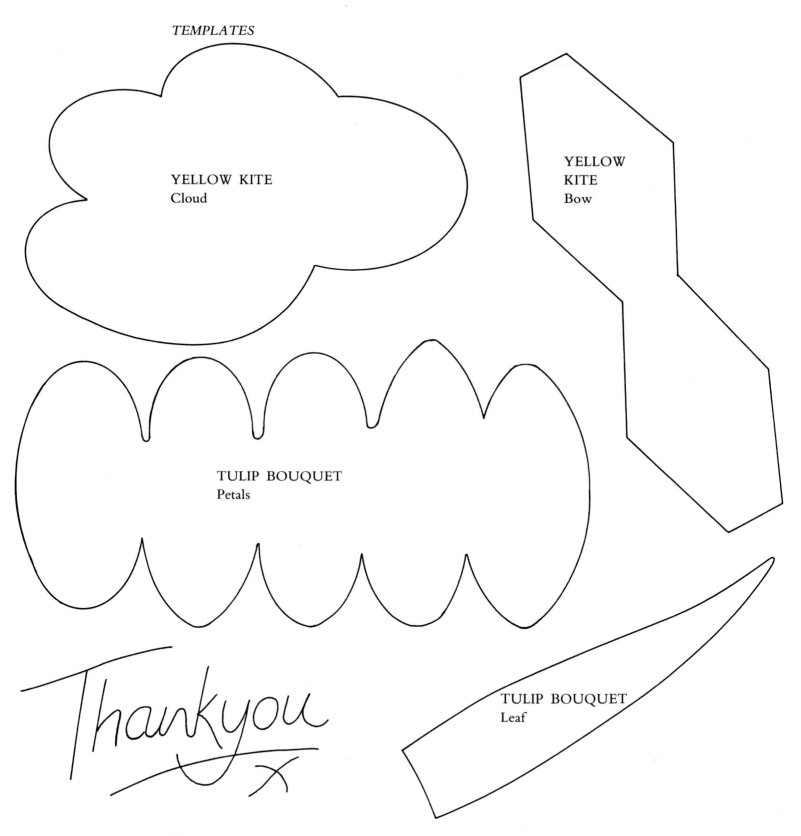

YELLOW KITE
Cloud

YELLOW
KITE
Bow

TULIP BOUQUET
Petals

TULIP BOUQUET
Leaf

Thankyou
x